IN THE CENTER OF THE FIELD

Poems

Also by Cynthia West from Sunstone Press.

Rainbringer, Poems
The New Sun, Poems

IN THE CENTER OF THE FIELD

Poems

Cynthia West

SANTA FE

Painting on front cover: The Fullness of Summer, Cynthia West, 2008
Prints on chapter title pages: Cynthia West, 2010
©2010 by Cynthia West. All rights reserved.

© 2011 by Cynthia West.
All Rights Reserved.

No part of this book may be reproduced in any form or by any electronic or mechanical means including information storage and retrieval systems without permission in writing from the publisher, except by a reviewer who may quote brief passages in a review.

Sunstone books may be purchased for educational, business, or sales promotional use. For information please write: Special Markets Department, Sunstone Press, P.O. Box 2321, Santa Fe, New Mexico 87504-2321.

Book and Cover design › Cynthia West
Body typeface › California FB
Printed on acid free paper

Library of Congress Cataloging-in-Publication Data

West, Cynthia, 1942-
  In the center of the field : poems / Cynthia West.
     p. cm.
  ISBN 978-0-86534-842-4 (pbk. : alk. paper)
  I. Title.
  PS3623.E84315 2011
  811'.6--dc23
                    2011036079

WWW.SUNSTONEPRESS.COM
SUNSTONE PRESS / POST OFFICE BOX 2321 / SANTA FE, NM 87504-2321 /USA
(505) 988-4418 / ORDERS ONLY (800) 243-5644 / FAX (505) 988-1025

DEDICATED TO JASON

CONTENTS

Preface   11
Acknowledgements   13

A NEW SKIN AWAITS: SPRING

   Watch Out   17
   The Dry Banks   18
   You Are Water   19
   The First Crocus   20
   The Gladness of Roots   21
   Silver Tunnels   22
   A New Skin Awaits   23
   Grey Wind   24

WHERE THE GRASS GROWS WIDE AS SKY
LATE SPRING, EARLY SUMMER

   Wild Seeds   27
   We Leap   28
   Sunday in the Lilacs   29
   Poor at Translation   30
   Children's Art   31
   The Sky Tide   32
   Sweet Water   33
   After It Has Flown   34

GATHERING HONEY: SUMMER

   Midsummer Afternoon   37
   This Brilliance   38
   Sharing the Swallows   39
   I Will Show You   40

Hands Inside My Hands   41
A Bird with Black Wings   42
Nothing Could Change   43
In the Green Warmth   44
By Letting Go   45
Before Your Leaves Fall   46

AS FAST AS THE ASPENS: LATE SUMMER, EARLY FALL

Painting the Rio Grande   49
Rain   50
Although I Live in Town Now   51
Apology to My Children   52
Never the Same   53
Faces   54
Sand Grains   55

TOO QUICK TO HOLD: AUTUMN

Food for the Winter   59
The Fool's Book   60
Journey to La Cieneguilla   61
Every Day I Walk Along the River   62
The Shore of Understanding   63
First Woman   64
Long Searching   65
In James' Orchard   66

GRASS BLADES, WHITE AS THE MOON
LATE FALL, EARLY WINTER

Hunting for Stones   69
Shoes Soaked with Rain   70
In the Absence   71

With Warm Soup   72
Dry   73
Rough Edges   74
A Song I'm Learning   75
To My Daughter   76
The Gathering of Ravens   77
No One Notices   78

IN THE DARK WELL: WINTER

Solstice   81
The Sun Fades Early   82
It Is Quiet Enough   83
In the Apple Tree   84
The Bones   85
Your Snakes   86
What If I Stop?   87
By the Winter Fire   88
So You Would Know   89
White Footprints   90

NO SENSE OF LOSS: LATE WINTER,
EARLY SPRING

Up Here Weaving   93
In the Moon's Tongue   94
Branches that Shelter   95
Joe   96
Addiction   97
No Sense of Loss   98
What She Knows   99
Inheritance   100
Asking the Snake   101
Spring Sledding   102

PREFACE

You have met Cynthia West many times before. Surely you will recognize her in *In the Center of the Field*: those summer clouds changing shape over the mountain, the singing colors of early autumn, the sounds of spring water rushing over stones, morning sunlight and shadows crawling along the abode wall, "water drops on iris".

Cynthia writes in her poem, "Mid-Summer Afternoon," "All my life I have wanted nothing more than to be in the garden, green wings beating, everything open to drink." She drinks from many gardens. Her poems have the touch of planting and harvesting daily life: the force enclosed in seeds and dirt. Nurturing is in her poems, the care and the gathering of succulence and essence in ripeness.

Her metaphors vibrate from living with memories of great joy, gray despair, of all she meets and inhales along her pathway. She is fearless in recognizing her many faces and voices.

As I read her poetry, I hear her ravens, climb her cottonwoods, wade her rivers, look for her mother, smell the food in her kitchen, walk in her grasses careful not to step on her crickets who have songs to sing to her.

In her poem, "By Letting Go," Cynthia discovers, "In the shadows there is no end to the views between leaves," It is here "In the Center of the Field" where I happily join Cynthia West shaping the clouds over Cerro Gordo hill behind her home.

She has given us words that can change the clouds in our hearts, forming them into how we might view, how we might listen to ourselves. The poetry of Cynthia West helps us to hear our own poems, our own voice, in the center of the field where we live and love.

James McGrath
Poet, Santa Fe, New Mexico
2011

ACKNOWLEDGEMENTS

My thanks to the publications in which the poems have appeared.

ANTHOLOGIES:

"In James's Orchard," *Looking Back to Place*, Old School Books, Albuquerque, edited by Susan McAllister, Becky Holtzman and Michaela Renz-Whitmore, 2008

"Every Day I Walk Along the River," *The Return of the River: Writers, Scholars and Citizens Speak on Behalf of the Santa Fe River*, edited by A Kyce Bello, Sunstone Press, 2010

"Watch Out" and "The Fool's Book," *A Feast of Fools Anthology*, edited by Melissa Guillet, Sacred Fools Press, 2010

REVIEWS:

"Apology to My Children," *Santa Fe Literary Review*, The School of Liberal and Fine Arts, Sudasi Clement, Poetry Editor, 2008

"Up Here Weaving," *Santa Fe Literary Review*, The School of Liberal and Fine Arts, Sudasi Clement, Poetry Editor, 2009

"Sand Grains and Journey to La Cieneguilla," *New Mexico Poetry Review*, Kathleen Johnson, Editor, Spring, 2010

"Poor at Translation" and "Nothing Could Change," *New Mexico Poetry Review*, Kathleen Johnson, Editor, Fall 2010

"To My Daughter," *Sin Fronteras Journal*, Richard Thomas and Wayne Crawford, Editors

A NEW SKIN AWAITS

SPRING

Watch Out

Fools wear green meadows, with birds
    in their hair. Animal friends inhabit
    parts of their bodies. The white cat

purrs in the belly, translating nights
    of stalking luminous limbs. The fool's house
    has walls which are diaries, grandparent's voices

written with blue ink. There are panels
    that retract, showing views long gone,
    mountains where loved ones lie buried

with stories in their bones. The rooms have hearths
    where fires are kindled to burn
    unnecessary boughs. The pruning continues

each spring until illusion is reduced
    to white ash. Empty rooms result, with space
    for the wind's tongue to drink. There are closets

of children's eyes ready to be worn
    on excursions to the river. They see the people
    who hide behind faces, find the ladders reaching

to the highest boughs. Watch out for the blue-green
    fools laughing in their gardens. They will lead you
    through doors that may not let you return.

The Dry Banks

Despite deep snows, the river isn't running.
    This Spring, standing in empty shoes,
        I can't find a path. The wind that blows falcons

has ripped my chest open, carried off the stories
    that made me understand. The tulips hang,
        colorless. When the current used to flow,

my friendship with the warm ground built a road
    to the land where I fit. My body matched
        the contours of the wind. I don't know how

I lost the map to the water that moves
    in my blood. Branches, sky, rocks, come around.
        Touch me. Show me how to return.

You Are Water

The river in spring murmurs with a voice
    made of rocks and reflected birds,
      "Be naked as I. No clothes can cover

my flowing, yet I wear the sun and the stars,
    the heat and the cold. There can be no past
    in streaming down the mountain, no loss
    in disappearing into the roots
    of green corn." "But," I say, "what happens

when drought withers your song?"
    "Step into me, place your head under my skin.
    Let me wash your mind of the angry bees

that make you forget. You are water,
    just as I. There is no more trouble in you
    than in the wind's blue laughter.
    There is no drying up in the truth

of the current, no glancing back,
    just wet stones mirroring
    the brightness of passing clouds."

The First Crocus

A trumpet from the stars,
    it yells on behalf of its kind,
    "We pierce any weight
    that presses on us. Nothing can stand

in our way. We thrust from the eyes of corpses,
    the mouths of murderers. We sprout joy
    for abused children, for women alone
    with no food. We bloom

in cesspools and graveyards,
    feed on whatever the soil holds.
    Blood, guts, decay,
    fuel our flames. Celebrating

the green fire that devours ice,
    we ripple up the hills painting light
    on grey-faced stones.
    We fill mouths with the birds that can fly."

The Gladness of Roots

Playing with the water drops on the iris
    I find you laughing back,
    or is it my own face
    infused with green? My hand stretching
    into the new-turned earth

reaches your pulse. I must touch
    all the parts of your body, your canyons
    where hawks mate in shadows,

your secret teeth that no one
    has ever seen. My fingers must roll your pearls,
    awakening the colors in petals. Let me hear
    you whisper your name
    in the yellow sheath unfurling,

your name, larger than anything I can know,
    your current, quickening my veins. Let me lie
    sweet in your alfalfa, seeded with sunlight,
    filled with the gladness of roots.

Silver Tunnels

When I planted
the heavenly blue morning glories
in a pot outside my window
    I dreamed of mouths spiraling open,
    translucent
    in late evening light. I slid
    through their lips in tunnels that led
    to the rising moon.

Although I don't have the maps
to those silver throats,
    the holes ripped in my skin by tears
    show me the way.

Warm and wet under straw mulch,
    the seeds germinate.
    Sprinkling them often, I watch
    for the first heart-shaped leaves.

I nail strings to the roof, tie them to poles.
    The vines reach up, forming a ladder
    I climb into the eye of the night.

A New Skin Awaits

The grandmothers I don't want to accept
    have woven their faces into my skull.
    Passing the beaver ponds, I can't help but join
    their reflections rippling grey and green.

Their tears in the melting snow guide me
    to the leaves that offer maps to the stone houses
    where my people struggled long ago. Ready to let
    my ears drown down in the bottom mud,

I hear my ancestor's cries. It means owning
    how I carry on their wounds. It means honoring
    the old ways. I wake covered with broken twigs.
    A fresh skin awaits, impatient from restraint, strong

as spring flood. Crafted over centuries, it unfolds,
    embroidered with deer and hawks, my name.
    I walk out wearing the meadows
    that welcome new-born birds.

Grey Wind

In past springs
    we tied poems
    to blossoming
    plum branches.

In the language of roots
    underground water flows,
    currents luring
    hidden gold.

In sharing song,
    we mingle.
    Wind washes change
    across the sky.

In the understanding
    between friends,
    fruit grows despite
    the frozen buds.

In the emptiness
    it is safe to uncover
    the sleeping doves
    we forgot.

WHERE THE GRASS GROWS
WIDE AS SKY

LATE SPRING, EARLY SUMMER

Wild Seeds

The woman who plants grasses
    speaks the language of the hills. Years of bending,
    listening, have given her the authority
    of stone. She presses wild seeds into the dust,

hand and soil one breath. Seasons in the wind
    have taught her the sound of the rain's feet.
    Standing tall before approaching clouds, she smells
    familiar signs, the silver undersides of leaves

turning their tongues to drink. There is no reason
    for her to labor day after day pulling weeds
    to allow room for sprouts. It is simply her work.
    When lightning splits the sky, she bows,

joining the rivulets which feed roots. Spiraling
    up stalks, swooping into cork-screw tufts,
    she is friends with the birds, the insects,
    the snakes, with the grasses greening the slopes.

We Leap

Our footsteps in the rain-wet sage
    pass over the brink
    where no trail goes. Blue juniper
    laden with berries whispers,
    "You've climbed beyond the fragile view
    you built to hold

yourselves apart." The undersides
    of clouds withdraw, leaving an eggshell sky.
    Hidden in a feathered cloak,
    we leap, flesh to flesh,
    soaring hawks above the cliffs.
    The edge of seeing drops. Smooth

as a water-worn stone,
    we raise antlers to circle the sun.
    Any slight breath could topple the grace
    with which wild grasses
    rest their blades on earth.

Sunday in the Lilacs

The spring night wraps us in her folded robes
until we vanish from our dreams. Blind, we can see
bright clouds weaving shadows with the stars.
The crescent moon rocks us in an ocean of belonging.

Disappearing even from our dreams,
we're hidden from the ravens circling overhead.
The crescent moon rocks us in an ocean of belonging.
In the safety of the lilacs the dark stops hunting us.

We're hidden from the ravens watching overhead.
We lie down together in good will.
In the safety of the lilacs the dark stops hunting us.
The small mice aren't afraid to gather 'round.

We float, submerged in black-skinned water,
friendship silvered by the moon. The small mice
aren't afraid to gather 'round.
We touch, soft as the wings of sleeping moths.

In the black-skinned water blind with moon,
we see bright clouds weaving shadows with the stars.
We touch, soft as the wings of sleeping moths.
The spring night wraps us in her folded robes.

Poor at Translation

The language of sparrows, the afternoon's play
    in the lilacs, the hum of branches,
        are lost if they are not told. The wind is a river

sighing in wild grass, speaking water
    in voices the leaves can drink. During the heat
    of the day, squirrels curled in burrows

understand what is being said. I listen
    to the grape vines strumming new fruit, to the
    squash blossoms opening. If I don't put

my ear to the ground, the murmurs, the rustlings,
    pass as if they never existed. If I don't hear
    down the throats of lilies, no one will know

their whispers or gather their golden talismans.
    Poor at translation, I fail the green stalks
    who have much to tell. I fail you,

who might not be able to continue
    without the stories of the plants.

Children's Art

Hopping over wheel weeds
    where the grass grows wide as sky, kids whirl into gopher holes
    laughing the blue morning down

to wake the roots.   This painting is a flicker's tail
    fanning across the sky, sheltering a nest.   Inside, baby birds
        dream yellow bells and green violins
    while the magician

forms their wings.   The stones bellow songs
    with huge orange voices like baked bread,
        fresh and steaming. Stones, warmth, table, voices,

winter sun and no more hunger.   Evening smells,
    painted purple, pool in the forks
      of poplar trees.   Sparrows hatch,
        fireworks from hidden eggs.   First flights

weave arcs across the darkening sky.   The streams
    are running with children's faces. Smiles, eyes,
        hands and feet leap ripples, catching
    clouds and trees.   Passing cars

on the road below are tiny because
    they're too loud to see.

The Sky Tide

Standing under the lilacs
    my shadow fills with fragrance
    until it expands
    into the sort of prayer
    that has more room than the seas.

Blue as the night,
    without bones or blood,
    I swim into the sky-tide
    that hushes the shores before dawn

Sweet Water

If I don't stop you from holding me
    the wheels everything is built of will show.
    The meanings hidden in apple blossoms
    will rise, bringing sweet water to drink.

The rings everything revolves on will show.
    Shadows in your eyes will turn to talismans,
    will soar, bringing sweet water to drink.
    Snakes will couple in the garden walls.

Shadows in your eyes will turn to talismans.
    It is not too late for golden iris to explode.
    Snakes will couple on the garden paths.
    Fields of new grass ripen tolling bells.

It is not too late for golden iris to divulge
    the meanings hidden under budding trees.
    Snakes will couple in the garden walls
    when I don't stop you from holding me.

After It Has Flown

Flickers perching on the power-lines
    call for help against the hard wind destroying
    their homes. One slams into the window,

falls with a broken neck. Gathering its warm feathers
    in my hands, it is as if the places of refuge
    have vanished. The moments fill the day

differently. How can I repeat the music the spring
    is made of, after it has flown to a country
    I can't find? The clouds thrust high.

Hanging the dead wings over my threshold,
    I remember to hear what is missing,
    to witness the shadows crossing the mountains.

GATHERING HONEY

SUMMER

Mid-Summer Afternoon

Soaked by the rain
I stand among the corn rows
    everything open to drink.

Shadows paint
    faces on the mountain,
      yet it remains the same.
Click bugs mate.
The patient canyon does not change.

Apricots fall, orange in the heat.
Hummingbirds throb,
    allowing the climbing beans
    to be heard.

Squash blossoms toll mid-summer,
    Sunday afternoon.
    Hollyhocks touch the sky.

All my life I have wanted nothing more
    than to be in the garden,
    green wings beating,
    everything open to drink.

This Brilliance

The sun at the peak of the year
    lets down a rope, knowing I will climb
    to feast on brilliance. It feeds me seeds of light

to transplant in the shelter of my garden.
    Although the fragments, separated from
    their blazing, seem pale here,
    I water them every morning at dawn,

watch their stalks strengthen. Cultivating
    these gifts is all the celebration I need.
    Bowing, bending, weeding, I come to believe

my saplings can flourish. Their new leaves
    and branches allow me the air I breathe,
    ripen the promise of fruit to nourish certainty
    on dark days. When thunder threatens,

I tie their trunks to poles. The sun at the height
    of fire understands, my only life is in raising
    harvests of light for people to eat.

Sharing the Swallows

Early mornings I climb down the arroyo
to discover the sun awakening
the granite edge. I want to know the cholla,
their thorns emerging from green flesh:
how they smell. Are the magenta blooms
formed in darkness? Why do the seed pods
resemble praying angels?

I ask to hear the words you don't say.
Do I need to peel back your skin
to uncover your treasury of stacked bills?
What water can I offer that would cause
your secret truths to sing?

I must locate the membrane
between the sky and the wind, enter,
dream awake the liquid sight
that swims green as trees. I plan to map it
for you so we can climb to the river together,
sharing the swallows; so we can meet
where the light and the dark
form granite and chollas.

I Will Show You

You held me, fed me with your aprons
    and lullabies. How could you know
    I was a stranger to your small porches,
    a traveler slipped from a huge mountain
    in the north? You thought I was like you,
    a garden that could easily be tended.

Held in the summer wind, I lay in clover,
    promising, "I will show you.
    I will make you see, even if your eyes
    are hoarded in closets with the gold
    that doesn't fill hope. I will grow my branches
    with the river you won't drink,
    until they rain floods
    that drown you in the sun.".

Mother, I keep painting pictures
    to describe what I mean, the lilies
    in the desert, the light that trees wear.
    You refuse to hear the ocean roaring
    under the kitchen floor.

I'm crying for the waters
    you won't let me share.
Mother, your unwillingness to see
    will drive me to explain
    long after you have gone.

Hands Inside My Hands

My road is paved with the prayers
    of the father I never knew,
    of the mother I never knew,
prayers I've never heard,
        which speak in my bones.

My eyes hold ways of looking
    I was not taught, views of mountains,
    views of rivers
        I've never seen.

Hands inside my hands
    remember the feel of faces I never knew.
Ears inside my ears, hear
    what the hummingbird sings
        while drinking of mid-summer.

The winds blow away the hours
    of the clock. I tend the fire in my blood,
    adding new wood
        to keep the blaze strong.

Many speak through me,
    my mother, my father, my bones,
    eyes, hands, hummingbirds, rivers,
    fire, blood and winds.
        My road is paved with prayers.

A Bird with Black Wings

We sit at the kitchen table pitting apricots
    for jam. The canyon crackles with the rain
    that blows away. Our sticky fingers

have learned the rhythm: split, squeeze, drop.
    There's nothing to say about how
    we'll never have this evening again,

no words for the elms listening outside. Working
    in good health, we're unconcerned
    about the headlights which could freeze us

at any moment, the truck which could smash us
    flat. Hearing a bird with black wings croaking
    in the distance, we're easy, thinking it isn't

summoning us. But making jam has nothing to do
    with keeping the ravens at bay. As jars line
    the shelves, clouds write our names with thunder.

Nothing Could Change

Ten of us ate dinner at the table every night,
    laughing, drinking, sure we were all
    the same. Sure that nothing could change.
    The stars wheeled above our old abode.
    Music poured out the windows. There was gladness
    in the valley. We thought family was a river
    that just kept watering more trees. We thought
    we knew each other.

The kitchen stands empty now, silent chairs
    facing each other across the printed cloth.
    The walls echo with stories. The colorful pictures
    have faded. We have left
    to follow our beliefs.

We move forward
    trying to get what we want. Some wait, confused,
    reading signs in unknown languages. Some wear
    other people's clothes. Each walks far from the rest,
    lost in a dream of joining that doesn't lead
    to a plain dirt road, a simple home.

In the Green Warmth, to Jason

A robin with a worm in her beak
    hops along the stone wall. She feeds
    babies nested in the grape leaves.
    I send her to you this summer afternoon
    to make you laugh as you sit alone
    watching cartoons. I've gathered the red smiles

of raspberries so you can stuff yourself
    until juice runs down your chin.
    There are birds I can't see in the trees,
    telling stories about the cloud shadows
    licking the mountain's face. Our rocks stand
    as we arranged them, the pirate ship
    in which we sailed to distant shores.

Close your eyes, see the palaces
    under the cucumber vines you planted.
    I'm gathering mint to make you tea.
    Smell its sweetness. Feel my hands
    soothing your hurt, fingers softer than sleep.

When you dream, place your hands into mine.
    We are scarlet runner beans flowering fireworks
    like the Fourth of July. Freedom blooms
    in your belly. Tea fills your glass.
    It overflows with the sun.
    In the warmth, our secret trees rest easy,
    in our green hands, no distance at all.

By Letting Go

Rising over Cerro Gordo hill,
    silver hands, open as wings, reflect

in the waters of my eyes, fold me
    into the play that gathers and dissolves,

not moored to any goal. Soft with the rains
    that ripen fruit, I am turning,

held by letting go. There is no journey
    but following the ringing edge of the day,

no breathing other than the boughs.
    There are many secrets only silence

can say. In the shadows, there is no end
    to the view between the leaves.

Before Your Leaves Fall

You, stranger in your own field,
    do you understand
    what the magpies are saying
    when they fly west at dawn?

Stranger to your own trees,
    do you know why the ice kills
    some and not others? Have you asked
    what warmth keeps certain vines
    producing grapes?

Have you gathered the secret
    for yourself? Stranger, fill your lungs

with the acrid breath
    of wild sunflowers. Fly like the goldfinches,
    stuffed with seeds. Remember,
    you have learned by bending,
    by weeding. Your fingers resemble
    cedar roots.
You swell like the corn after rain.

Grandmother, before your leaves fall,
    recognize that you wear rainbows
    the way the mountains do.

AS FAST AS THE ASPENS

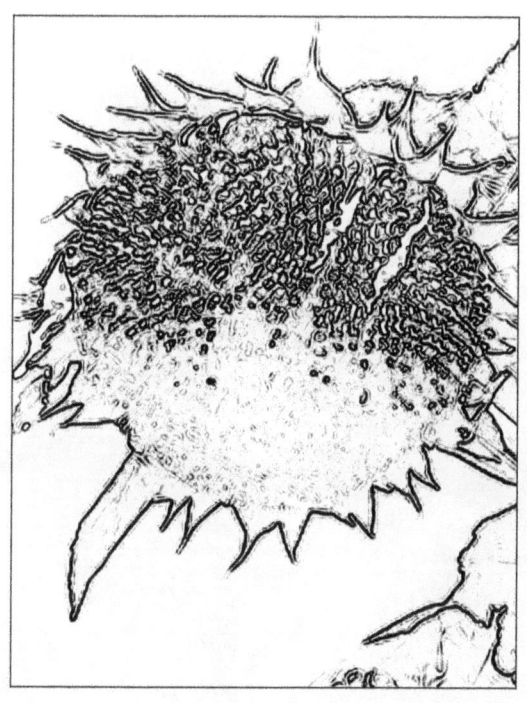

LATE SUMMER, EARLY FALL

Painting the Rio Grande

On a day turning toward fall, there is no edge
    where the ripples end and the mud begins. The mesas,
    ripened by the moon, unfurl blue shadows.

Under the Russian Olive, my brushstrokes touch
    the yellow chamisas, the asters. Matching hue to hue,
    I add the quick wings of Canadian Ducks

migrating south. Mounds of grass gladden the banks.
    I harvest beauty onto canvas, against the cold bear
    waking in the stars. A flock of stellar jays

sweeps into a cottonwood. Bright strands of sky,
    they weave the season's ending which will rise
    like bells of winter smoke above the villages.

Rain

Come water my fields, dark running clouds,
    thick horse clouds, pale shadow clouds
    heavy with gifts. I'm standing on the road

worn by the steps of my people. I'm following
    the song trail carved in the mesa since
    the first sun warmed the earth. I'm spreading

a path of pollen for you. Rain people, let your breath
    fill the deep corn roots. Let your lightning
    ignite the kernels. Let your thunder ripen my fruit.

I'm holding up the bowl of my body,
    asking you to drink the white of the dawn,
    the red of the south, the turquoise west,

the black north, the up and the down. Come,
    feed on my colors until you burst

Although I Live in Town Now

Today the geese fly south
    bearing summer away on their wings.
    I stretch my hands to catch the cries

they let fall. Although I live in town now,
    with no tree to hold their sounds, I hear them
    in my sleep. The smell of dust raised by thunder
    lies stored in my dreams
    as well as fields of ripe corn.

Sticks tied with four colors touch the moon.
    Although I live in town now,
    my dance-ground waits where I hide it,

under the blue bowl of August painted
    with the sunflowers of my people.
    Although the stream by the highway

has dried up, I save a basket of clouds
    to sing into rain. I keep the ancient bowls
    to harvest the peaches. When I visit my shelves
    in winter, I will have plenty to eat.

Apology to My Children

Today I'm answering for all the caring
    I never gave. While I weeded the garden
    your young voices called for my arms.

My doors didn't know how to close.
    All those visitors sat in your chairs talking
    over your cries. I served them

platefuls of enchiladas, beans and corn.
    In the kitchen garlanded with chiles,
    the coffee was always warming

on the stove. Downstairs, in the basement
    beneath my smile, I longed to hold you,
    but I'd never learned how.

Today, I'm answering by pouring you
    all you ever wanted. I call you,
    stare into your sad grey eyes, only to find

they are cold moons risen far beyond
    our small hill. Long ago you gave up
    sitting by the dahlias out front, waiting

for me to take your hand.
    Why did I, who never arrived for you,
    suppose you would never leave?

You've moved away, further than if
    you'd hid, farther than my cries
    can reach. Calling up your ladders,

I'm gathering everything I wish
    had happened, offering it to the absence
    where you once stood.

Never the Same

Ask the grasshoppers gnawing
    the wild asters

        if they can catch the shadows
        that will never repeat.

Every afternoon thunder
    sounds different views.

        Dahlias unfurl faster than water over stone,
        impossible to touch.

When the sound of your voice
    falls from my fingers

        it leaves me holding
        the husk of summer.

Dry and breaking, I shake it,
    coaxing seeds I save to warm the snow.

Faces

When thunder hides the moon my branches
    drink the dark, swelling
    into a river of stars. The school

that waits folded in sleep
    tolls shadowy bells. I've grown gourds
    for gathering the water that is too quiet to see.

Swallowing the cold mouth of night,
    I am many faces who know how to be leaves,
    many sorrows that lead like ladders

to the land where tears cease. A giant trunk,
    I am rings circling out from the center, each born
    for no reason but the offering of fruit, of seed.

Sand Grains

Here in the center of the field,
    in the circle of my parent's ashes, it is clear
    they have never left. The sunflowers stand

calling the thunder. The valley, so hot it melts,
    rises to meet the galloping wind.
    The daily sameness has blown away

taking the laughing asters on a ride.
    Petals swirl, leaving air trails that define
    the grey sinking, the growing pressure

of the clouds. The waters gathering
    from hidden places unfurl dark wings.
    My mother and father remain, etched

on the shrouded mountain. They speak
    in the hard rain pocking the dust.
    They are sand grains worn from stone

trickling through my fingers. There is no way
    to stop their flow,
    no aloneness in the storm.

TOO QUICK TO HOLD

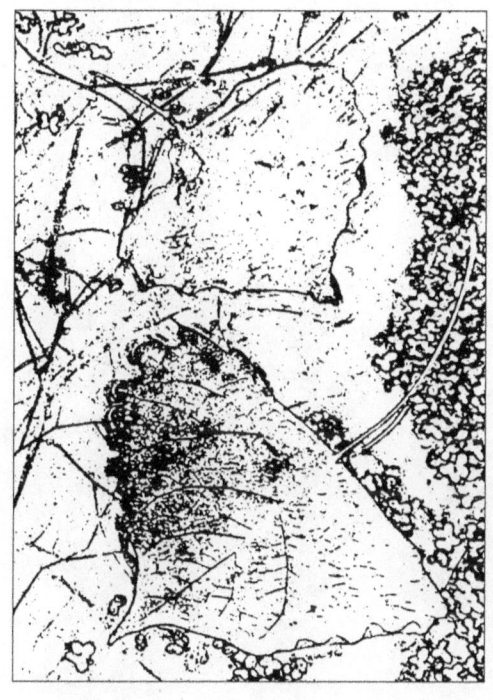

AUTUMN

Food for the Winter

Spinning clay prayers
      on the wheels of days, I craft vessels, fire them
      in the sun that doesn't set. I fill my bowls

with spirals and the blue jays that call
      in wild plum thickets. Saplings I planted
      years ago offer fruits to pack

in my jars. Honey from delphiniums is stored,
      as well as the thorns of loss, the ashes
      of loved ones I've buried in the field.

The paint on my bowls is ground of tears
      the colors of earth. Giving you rich food,
      I ask you to eat the silence gathered

by the river. I've prepared feasts, some light,
      funny as family nights around the table,
      some hard with the cold that nothing

can fill. I come bringing the whole forest
      so you can be one of the trees.

The Fool's Book

When gusts blow the windows wide
    night hawks fly holding cards in their beaks,
        queens, jokers, aces, each illustrated
        with dreams
        drawn in a bucket from the well
            beyond waters.

Laughter lies scattered on the floor, moon-seared,
        bright.
    When the sheets turn to waves
I dive, gathering images,
        fitting them to cavities in my flesh.

Each one has a voice announcing news so strange
    I must recognize it as my own,
            hidden under rocks where I can't find it
            even when the lights go on.

Come in, I say, though they are already rooted,
        growing like trees. Here is the tight-rope walker
            wearing mercury, balancing
            yesterday and tomorrow on a long pole.
    Here is the collector of broken wings,
        sewing, mending, gluing.

Too many to fit in my book, the guests who have moved in
    sprawl all the way to the horizon.
        The pages resound with cheering.

Journey to La Cieneguilla

Along the road,
    the skeletons of wild sunflowers
    rest arm in arm,

smiling at a job well done.
    Along the road,
    fields of pigweed sigh.

I have never seen
    their magenta stalks before today.
    One chime of the clock

doesn't stop the apples
    from dropping. I have never seen
    how old the bark is, how strong

from many winters warming
    unborn fruit. Before today
    I never guessed that the wild asters

are earth's eyes closing into sleep.
    Along the road, the afternoon
    disappears beneath my tires.

Until today, I have never touched
    the small seeds
    which are larger than the sky.

Every Day I Walk Along the River

It is silver coin, rich with the rush
    of water over stones.

It is a feast of magpies, slicing
    black and white ladders to the sun.

The warmth is not hidden behind clouds.
    As my feet crush brittle weeds, I smell roses
    with bees drinking music until they fall.

Friends warn me not to go alone,
    but if they came, their traffic would drown out
    the flutes in the rushes along the shore.

Every day I bring my red wagon to gather
    the secrets that bloomed in the night.
    There are loaves and apples, wine as well.

The Shore of Understanding

We're candles singing in a circle
    around the feet of turtle earth.
    The light of our voices
    reveals the vastness of the stars.

Invitations were sent to us
    who bet everything we had and lost,
    who continue to play
    after the house has repossessed
    all we own.

We roll our dice through the night
    gathering honey to feed the orphans.
    The need to win no longer prevents
    our hands from reaching the cards
    that seal wounds.

We chant on the shore
    of understanding, weaving the roots
    and the heavens into nets
    to catch those
    who can't fly.

Dawn eats our small flames,
    the ones we release
    as easily as water.

First Woman

Sometimes, awake in my sleep, I see
    her swimming made of stars. Other nights
    her body is seeds and grasses. The wind,

a blue heron with wide wings, sweeps me
    into her, my mother made
    of cornmeal and blood, the one

who formed me, the one who gathered the waters
    to feed my roots, the one whose rivers
    I have planted in my daughters, the one

who sings. Sometimes when I am awake
    she gives me the voices of cedar and sage,
    songs hidden in branches that build

ladders to new eyes. Sometimes when I sit
    in the golden fields she lulls me with a dream.
    I must follow her tracks all the way home

to the valley between her breasts.
    When I have climbed that far,
    she brings me honey to eat.

Long Searching

The deer hide in golden fields
    across the river, blended in grasses
    and wind. Shots ringing on the ridge-line

will not find their liquid eyes. Sliding
    through dry stalks, I gaze at the sky
    waiting for horns to cleave

the sea of wheat. Weighted seed heads
    stand stark, highlighted against
    indigo shade. What I am looking for

refuses to be seen. Tired, I lie down,
    cheek to the roots. Flocks
    of laughing crows hurtle south.

They are too loud to find the slow swish
    of silver hooves on gold. Keeping still,
    surrounded by warm breathing,

by large ears ringed with black, I am
    the hearing that comes with no sound,
    the seeing that opens as evening falls.

In James' Orchard

Chasing up trunks, squirrels flash, disappear.
New-born swallows hide
    in green branched caves.
Round apple-smiles breathe a blush
    onto my skin, a water
    quenching long-held thirst.

I couldn't be here today unless I'd left
    my old maps out to peel in the sun.
Bleached of their certain colors, the pages have
    cracked, allowing the ringing of stars
    to promise rain. In this orchard,

the mourning doves settle in my lap, sensing
    harm has faded, along with importance.
There is nothing to be remembered
    in this rustling cavern of friends.
I haven't done anything to deserve
    these leaves
    or these ants laboring home
    under burdens larger than themselves.

GRASS BLADES, WHITE AS THE MOON

LATE FALL
EARLY WINTER

Hunting for Stones

When the branches let go their leaves it is hard
    to move my feet through the mud.
    When cold shrinks the light, few shadows
    mark the path. When green ice closes the pond

to the touch of sky, the sorrows of others
    are a sinking grayness, a burden that presses
    down. The thickets open when I become
    a child crawling on my belly. Hunting for stones,

just the right ones to build a circle of thanks,
    allows me passage through a door
    that seems too small. Stained glass appears,
    glowing between branches, lifting the heaviness.

There are warm birds here. When their eyes
    meet mine, I hear nothing but the laughter
    of bells, the calling home
    that makes distance lose all sense.

Shoes Soaked with Rain

There is no loneliness
    in this orchard
       with the crickets as friends.

My home lies in a garden
    that frost can't stop
    from blooming.

Along the path in the field,
    I rake leaves,
    my shoes soaked with rain.

Waning year, I walk with you
    through the thicket.
    Clouds rest in the folded hills.

On a cold morning before dawn,
    all around me, grass blades,
    white as the moon.

In the Absence

Without my rows of marigolds
    I am cold earth,
      an empty cup holding snow.
      There are no ducks up the canyon,
      no sounding finches, no towhees

in the thickets. Have they hidden
    under the shadows
      to stay warm? The sun swings low,
      filling my footsteps with gold. The deer
      return. Secrets that didn't show before

are glimpsed hanging in branches
    where the wind
      let them fall. In the absence
      left by the warmth flying south,
      the full moon can speak at last.

With Warm Soup

Can I tell how sad she was,
    making me breakfast
    that I didn't want?

Her nervous hands, darning
    my socks, what did I care
    to receive? Her rapid steps,

up the stairs with warm soup
    when I was sick, I never thanked
    her or noticed the lines

growing down the corners of
    her mouth. It hurts too much to say
    how hard she tried to please.

After I left, her empty gaze at the window
    followed my shadow
    until it disappeared from sight.

The evenings fell blue as she played
    the Moonlight Sonata to no one,
    her love rising, seeking me.

Dry

Forty years ago, keeping up the smile,
                wanting to be liked,
                each evening weeping in the field,
                I didn't find relief. Always busy,
keeping up the smile, I housed visitors
                who demanded the mother
                I couldn't be, sucked me dry.

Lips to cold stone, I inhaled tobacco smoke,
                not the kiss that lured me here.
Trash piled under the old Rival wood-stove,
                kindling that gave no warmth.

Keeping up the smile, I ate bitter herbs,
                ashes in my mouth. Dull days trudged
                one after another to the wringer washer,
                diapers, no lilacs, no release.

Storms swallowed the rising sun. A captive mother,
                keeping up the smile,
                begging softness from the walls,
                I let the black clouds steal my face.

Rough Edges

Clumsy, ugly, never done,
    slow, sick, I can hardly move, carrying
    the family on my back. Frustrated, I haul
    the garbage, endure frozen chrysanthemums
    and the muddy road. A vision I lost

of us sharing roses
    with the blue sky pouring
    into one another's eyes

leads me to keep on. Every day
    among the same wilted flowers,
    the children, the roof-leaks, the bills, I work
    for my hope to come true. How tired I rush,
    greying, breaking, out of breath
    from racing toward a sun
    that never seems to near. I don't have time

to notice that we have become the garden
    with the blue sky pouring, shining through
    rough edges, through each other's tears.

A Song I'm Learning

The peach tree has grown old, its bark mapping
      the passage of years. In November
      it releases orange leaves to the wind,
      a language I'm learning. Violet buds burst

from bare branches, houses to shield
      blossoms from the snow. Roots deep
      in the earth pump water up magenta limbs,
      honoring the full moon. Far from fluent,

I repeat the secrets the shadows dance
      on frozen ground. Voicing the sounds
      of greenness, of sweetness, of letting go,
      I gather enough notes to weave a song.

To My Daughter

I held your small hand,
： read to you,
： ： turned you step by step ： to learn my dance,
： ： ： the one I thought best for you.

I lifted your face up, ： up, like the rising branches
： until I thought you could swallow the sun
： ： by yourself. ： I admired
： the hopes I'd pasted on you, ： planning
： ： for you to complete

my idea of fruit. ： Too busy whirling
： to my own music ： I didn't notice
： ： my clouds had failed ： to provide
： ： ： the sort of rain you could drink.
： ： Little I guessed your tree
： ： ： needed another earth

than mine, ： another water
： to grow strong ： against
： ： the killing frosts.

The Gathering of Ravens

Pieces of the night with wings,
    where they fly
    the darkness shines blue.

They fill every tree.
    The hills provide bleachers
    for thousands. Wild cawing dissects

the wind, stitches it back
    into new patterns. They gather
    from every direction, inking the sky

with meaning. As I pass, they startle,
    weaving me into their black water.
    Shadows that open mountains,

that lift the naked willows,
    their indigo cries predict
    more than the coming of snow.

No One Notices

After you turn sixty,
    when people think you don't matter anymore,
    you're free to unpack the old fool's hat you crafted

of corn-silk and spider-webs. You dyed strands
    of ancestral laughter with silver reflections,
    stitched them to a cap,
    created antlers of light. If you had flaunted it,

you'd have been put away, along with the others
    who dance outside the mind. Now that no one notices,
    you can wear it to the market. Now that no one listens,

you can turn up the volume of bird whistles
    calling the sunrise. The cereals are more likely
    to hear than the shoppers. Forget your heavy coats,

don instead the turquoise tongues you gathered
    from butterflies while everyone thought
    you were succeeding
    at business. Retired, you can live openly

in the house you built of earth and water,
    of sunlight and stars.
    An old fool, you can sing by the fire.

IN THE DARK WELL

WINTER

Solstice

On the night before the full moon,
    falling into the long, black, cold,

I begin,
    no arguments left,
    no more tears.

With the deer and the silver birds
I bow
    on frozen grass lit almost as bright as day.
I begin the winter
    no longer who I liked to think I was.
I begin the winter lying in the stars.

This is my body
    washed of imagined colors. It is a wheel
    that rolls in circles,
    a song catcher filling with the truth
    the west wind brings.

These are my hands,
    shining cups, new,
    unfamiliar with the wine they pour
    on the sinking fields.

I begin,
    an empty shadow.
    I enter the dark time
    made of light.

The Sun Fades Early

As the storm rages, I sweep evergreen
    scraps off the floor. The windows shine,
    garlanded with cedar and piñon.
    They are eyes, keeping watch through

the drab afternoon for the first ray
    of longer light. In the dark well of the year
    time stretches, allowing silver moments
    to soothe my face. Each breath contains

more than I understand. I work
    through the day straightening stones
    along the path, spreading blankets
    of golden straw on the sleeping flowers.

Like the trees, I find relief, allowing
    the wind to roost in the spaces between
    bare limbs. When the sun fades early
    and deep blue stains the sky,

I wait for the winter stars.
    Long ago, I thought I had to fight.
    As blackness falls, it is more than enough
    to welcome the return of the sun.

It Is Quiet Enough

In winter when the cedars hunch down,
    doors open in thickets, colored lights shine.

White wings stretching across the sky
    are not as wide as the silence

that allows forgotten heat to rise. Shivers burst
    into long-ago firesides where whispered kisses

lit our skin. In winter when nothing is happening
    it is quiet enough for the unseen to return.

When time stops between one flame and the next,
    snow covers the tracks of the deer.

In the Apple Tree

With the leaves fallen,
    a nest is visible.

Last night it held
    the snow and the stars.

When morning melted the ice,
    water drops vanished in the earth,
    one by one.

The birds have flown.
    The nest will blow apart.

The Bones

No soaring parts the frozen air;
    no wind stirs. The ashes give me eyes
    which contain the sight of the mountain.

When I gaze through them, the bones
    of the stories I once believed
    cover the field with white. In the murmur

of melting ice the light is hard to bear,
    a vacancy where breathing has ceased,
    a pure water void of sound.

There is nothing in my room
    but the year awaiting birth. I hold
    the feathers it will need to fly.

Your Snakes

There's much to be seen
    if you kneel in the mud, pry up rocks,
    peer into the dark. Face it, if you

could have endured the sky's blue gaze,
    you'd never have sickened
    from hiding. If you hadn't lowered

your eyes from the seasons' turning,
    you would not have grown blind.
    Your mouth wouldn't have an ugly twist

from refusing celebration. Your veins
    wouldn't have burst from holding
    your thunders captive. Stretch your fingers

into the shadows under the stone. Feel
    your snakes waiting to strike. Allow
    your hand to meet their writhing.

What If I Stop?

Lunging as if I could catch it,   arms, legs flailing,
    I grab at my shadow thrown monstrous up the wall
    by swaying lanterns.   The drunken wind

      smashes plastic chairs.   If I could rip
        my head free, I'd hurl my fury
so hard it would break.   There's no food
    behind these doors,
      no allure in these eyes. In the jumbled bobbing

is it my rage   that annihilates my brain
    or is it I?

Baggage of harm, bric-a-brac, ridiculous trophies
      block the way.   If I shed my frenzy
        could I feed the flutter of a single finch
    with a clean sky its wings could savor?

By the Winter Fire

Sixty-five years, I've dreamed
    by the winter fire,
    with the smell of wood-smoke,
    eyes carried far by the flames.

My house is clean, swept,
    lit by a candle. Flowers bloom on the table.
    The ones that don't fade.
    The ones I have grown.

The earth walls hold stories.
    In the kitchen pots bubble on the stove,
    fragrant with corn and chile.

Out the window the small desert view
    has taught me the ways of water.
    Dipping and diving with the swallows,
    I count the waves
    found only in a still heart.

So You Would Know

My ashes rest in the river of events
    that don't return, in the tracks
    of the fallen years. When I was here with you

time seemed wide, generous with green leaves.
    It was easy to postpone admitting I wore
    false colors that storms would blow away.

I collected needles and threads, meaning
    to teach you how to sew your feet to this valley,
    so you could walk with the birds in joy.

Snow penetrates my eyes, blinding me. Quick,
    let me touch your cheek. Here is the bundle
    I gathered for your weeping hours.

It holds rainbows to wrap your fears.
    I wanted to explain the ways of feathers
    so you would know how to use the wings

I wove to carry your prayers. I meant
    to bring you dreams filled with bright grains
    so you would understand why I sing

with stars in my hair. When you kneel
    in the cold mud which has swallowed me,
    you will find the roses that do not go out.

White Footprints

Walking out today
    on snow that crunches loudly
    I am a passenger
    at the beginning of the field
    I've called mine
    for thirty years
    with little knowledge of the earth
    that carries me.

Holding a lifetime of prayers
    under the morning star
    it is hard to take breath
    in cold this deep.

My days bow
    grateful to step
    out of the wind to kneel
    warm beside roses and candles.
    In the black eyes of flames
    no loneliness
    only the sea.

No longer an abandoned child writing,
    "I will be good if you will like me,"
    over and over on my mother's face
    I am a woman who gives
    white footprints
    back to the snow
    steps that no one need see
    invisible circles
    in a little-known canyon
    whirling around the sun.

NO SENSE OF LOSS

LATE WINTER
EARLY SPRING

Up Here Weaving

Nobody values the dark at the top of the hill
    after the moon has set.

She harvests it anyway, stirs it
    in her basket of feathers
    until it sings of the undersides of stones
    and of skeletal cicadas left unseen.

If anyone knows she is up here weaving
    with the fingers of dead piñons,
    they don't care.

Silently, she gleans the bitter snow
    in which her scars find rest.
        With black ears and eyes she listens to the wind,
    crawls down the cedar roots.

Finding food in bark scattered
    on the stones, she grows trees from emptiness.
    With dry stalks she forges sounds, scrapings
    too faint to be heard. The sky gathers her,

whispering, "Yours are invisible songs,
    the kind no one pays money for,
    the kind that keep me turning
    after the moon has gone."

In the Moon's Tongue

When you want to know why I'm not here
    I have to explain I live elsewhere, in the shadows
    of rabbits hastening across the dusk,
    in the moon's tongue comforting the husks

of frozen plums. While you think I'm interested
    in your talk, I'm wondering why I left the ocean,
    why I press against the cold wind
    when I could be floating in the silver eyes of fish.

I don't understand why the land of dry stones
    has called me to dig wells. My broken cup
    can still hold the night's waters. I'd offer them
    to you if you would drink.

Branches that Shelter

The book I'm writing is grown of trees drawn
    in green-ink with a pen. The lines are
    flowing sap, blooming branches that shelter

faces from high winds. When dust-devils
    rip the apricot blossoms, the eyes on the pages
    keep smiling, the hands remain touching,

the roots drink water deep under stone.
    The images are talking leaves with lessons
    so simple they halt the storms. They form

a tunnel leading to the friendship that withstands
    spring snows. Mountains and valleys melt ice
    into fertile mud. An aspen forest, my story

neither finishes nor stops, but releases
    new seeds to sprout, year after year.

Joe

The days of his life,   photos developed
 through the eyes of drugs, lie stacked
 ready for the trash. You can see his feelings,
  negatives on glass.   Dark shapes flee

into others, unable to stop long enough
  to be known. Chemistry you don't understand
  adhered his nerves
  to these shifting window panes. Sunlight streams through,

projecting shadow dramas
  on his bed. If you can't find meaning,
  try listening for running water weaving notes
  too high to hear.   Crying for his wasted promise,

are you sure he failed?   Can you claim
  he squandered his coins
  on losing horses? He may have stored
  treasure on these transparent slides.

He may have been too sad to tell you, fearing
  you wouldn't want his gifts.

Standing on the Rio Grande Gorge Bridge
  you watch   the white specks of his ashes float
  all the way down to the river. The nesting eagles
  will keep an eye on Joe.

Addiction

She's a power engine vacuuming all
    into her spell. She's hammering, pounding,
    luring us into her wasteland to become
    blue flies. Her insatiable hunger

gnaws our innards leaving shadows,
    red blood bursts, fruit dying on trees. Like a potter
    at the wheel she forms what she touches, spinning,
    turning liquid eyes to glass, warm skins

to bitter shells. She hates her creations
    waiting tamely for the kiln. The dark fire brings
    no release, no interest in the dolls she'll shove out
    to gather charcoal in her fields. Cursing,

she demands the people she can't consume, the ones
    who haven't been swallowed by her smile, who refuse
    to poison the finches, who pull weeds to make room
    for wild grass. She wants the fugitives, the ones exiled

and alone who remember how to laugh, the ones no one
    understands, who talk to raindrops and moths. She needs
    the ones who feel they're a mistake,
    who wish they'd been born with wings,

the ones she can never catch.

No Sense of Loss

Under a racing sky
it is strange to lie on the shore

panting among sprouts and grasses.
What's left behind doesn't matter.

I've no sense of loss
for the years wasted building walls

that ruined the view. Low in the mud,
new-hatched, skinless, I am

one liquid eye. Dead so long,
you might suppose I'd forgotten how

to slither on my belly
through the greening water roots.

What She Knows

After fire sweeps the riverbed one spider
    crawls out from under a scorched rock
    into a world no longer her own. No swollen buds
    spill sap, no friction blows

the limbs green. Charred skeletons shake
    like brittle nerves. Black against the ashes,
    she hums the grey fluid which starts
    her weaving strands. With the usual landscape

wrecked, she casts glances at the cinders,
    ripples eight legs in patterns.
    It is what she knows.
    Despite the destruction of her dancing ground

she spools a rhythm of thread, silk she glues
    to charcoal twigs. It's a song, all she has.
    Her art is the same as the web which holds
    the stars in place. She is the last one.

Plugging her belly into the center of the web,
    she erupts with eggs.

Inheritance

The apple trees have become songs
     from my son's pruning. Not that much wood
     has been removed, just the right amount

to sculpt the limbs in symmetry. What else
     should he be doing than interacting with trunk,
     sky and sap? What art is more important

than guiding branches into the shapes
     that best produce fruit? The goldfinches
     smile at him. What more could he profit

laboring for a wage? What better occupation
     than sawing, gently removing
     unnecessary boughs? Balanced on high,

he holds the clouds in his head, not small thoughts,
     but the wind's pure breath. Inhaling the scent
     of fresh-hewn wood, he soothes the cuts

with his palm. He could excel at many jobs.
     Did he learn from me the wild
     and precious work that goes unseen?

Asking the Snake

With my ear to the stone wall
    I am listening
    for your stirring. The warmth

that opens buds too soon
    has started your song.
    Because I have lost my way

to the underground river, I ask you
    to show me. Teach me the words
    of your waking-up rhythm

so I can breathe with the green roots,
    ride the red sap to the centers
    of blossoms. Electrify

my branches with the surge
    that demands the kiss of the light.
    Look, I'm digging a hole

to bury my fear. In the moon
    of white daffodils,
    fill my hands with fire.

Spring Sledding

I'm the fool on the roadside putting on a show.
    Few pause to throw coins
    as I teach the leaves
    how to drink the sun.
Who wants the cruelty of unfolding
    from a warm sheath into ice?

In spring snow, I sled down hills.
    Brilliance sears,
    leaving no edges
    to my shadow.
Spontaneous combustion thrusts me off
    the brink before the ground
    rushes up hard. No one can stop me.
    Falling is the way to find
    the place in between,
    the hollow where my body fits.

You could say I've held my skull up
    to the flames
    until it holds nothing
    but houses for wild birds.

Seeking higher ridges
    from which to soar, I extend the gap
    before the crash.

In the orchard with no time,
    eyes wait to be picked from branches,
    sight that reveals people
    as I've always known them to be:
    bounding blue with no end.

Wearing my old fool's hat,
    on the side of the road, I juggle
    the miracles few have time to witness,
    offer free tickets for return.

This book of poetry is printed on acid-free paper.
The typeface is Californian FB

In 1938, Goudy designed California Oldstyle, his most
distinguished type, for University of California Press.

In 1958, Lanston issued it as Californian.

Carol Twombly digitized the roman 30 years later for California;
David Berlow revised it for Font Bureau with italic and small caps;
Jane Patterson designed the bold. In 1999, assisted by Richard Lipton &
Jill Pichotta, Berlow designed the black and the text and display series.

www.ingramcontent.com/pod-product-compliance
Lightning Source LLC
Chambersburg PA
CBHW022007100426
42738CB00041B/810